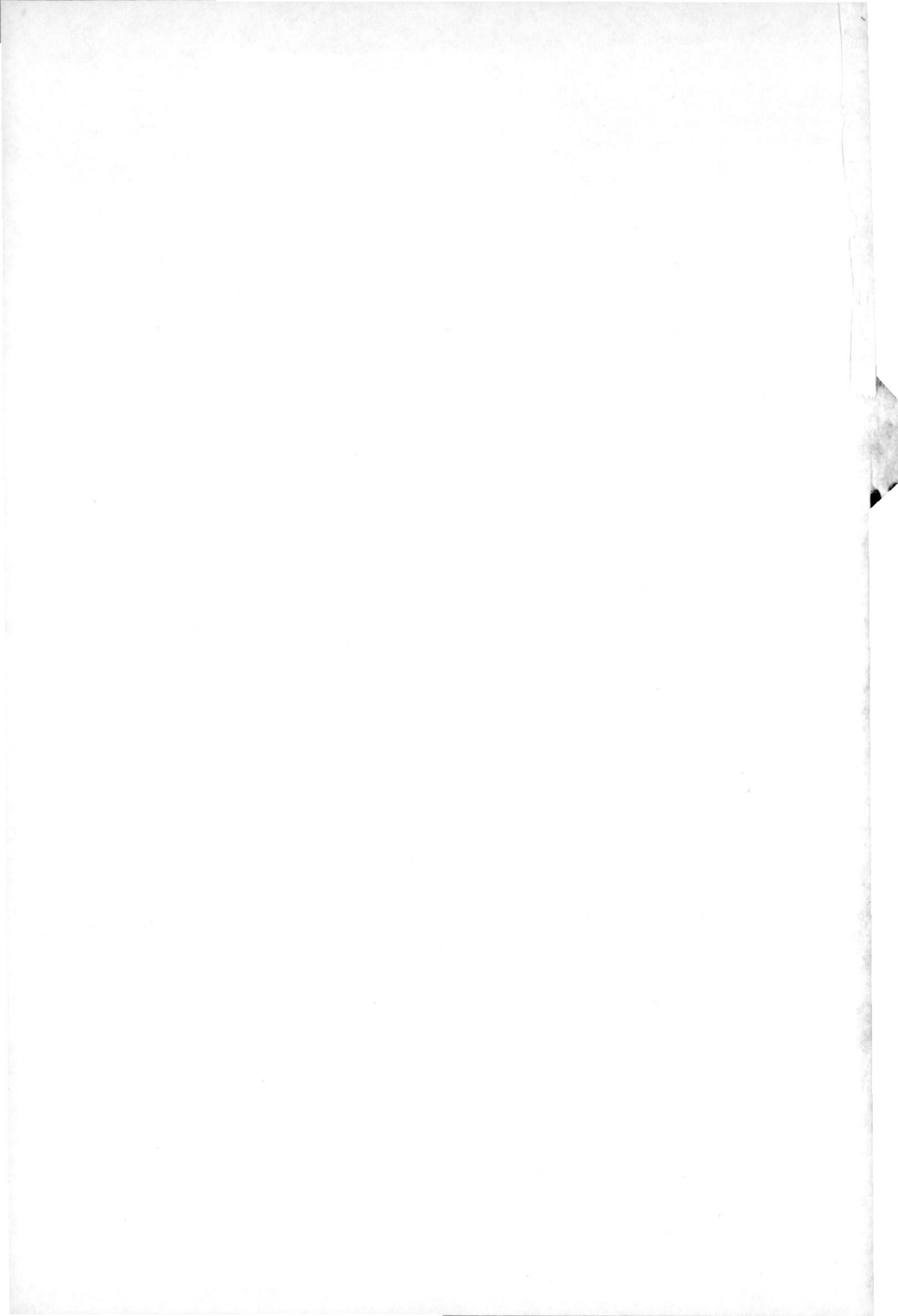

Verse Sketches
Of The Lake Poets

Verse Sketches
Of The Lake Poets

By

John Peaston

First Published in Great Britain in 2000
by ProPrint, an imprint of
   Wheatmill Publishers
   Wheatmill House, 7 New Wood Lane,
   Blakedown, Worcs DY10 3LD

A Catalogue record for this book is
available from the British Library

ISBN: 0 9536207 1 9

Typesetting and layout
Printed and bound by ProPrint Ltd, England

To Barbara, Jane and Anne

CONTENTS

THE FERRYMAN OF WINDERMERE

'Come, Ferryman of Windermere,
I needs must row into the cloud
Beyond the shore, beyond the mere,
Where souls may hide, or disappear
Not to the Earth, enclosed in shroud,
But free to feel the Lakeland air
And with our forebears Paradise to share.'

'I, Ferryman of Windermere,
Must know your name, must know your Mind
Before the Lake without a fear
I row you far, or row you near.
What is your name, what is your kind
Before we share the dying light
And row the waters through the coming night?'

'I, Ferryman of Windermere,
Am Spirit of the Poet's Word
And all who lived and flourished here,
Whose tender words extract a tear
And see emotive vision blurred
With images can scarce restrain
A repetition of the Bard's refrain.'

'Then, Spirit of the Poet's Word,
Step lightly now, step lightly here,
And I will row as fleet as bird
Might fly, had darkness not occurred
Before his wings widespread appear:
Will row into the dark and haze
And take your Spirit through the nightly maze.'

So sat the Poet's Spirit still
Nor feared the dark, nor feared the sea,
As Ferryman the evening chill
Rowed through the cloud, rowed with a will
Until it seemed, afar to lea
A paler shore began to show
Whereon a light transcendent seemed to glow.

And from the dark the boat appeared
And drifted slow to sandy shore,
Through hazy dark the rower neared
The lighted shore, which neither feared,
Until as closer came yet more
The gliding visitors to land
The noiseless bow rose 'printed in the sand.

Without a Word, without a sigh,
Alighted silent ghostly tread
As Spirit left the margin by
The moveless bow, the tide-wrack nigh
And sought, yea sought the living Dead,
As Ferryman of Windermere
Remained aboard, alone, and pale, and sere.

The Spirit of the Poet's Word approached
A clearing close to gently soughing seas
And there he saw, where waters close encroached
A glade within a forest deep of beech,
A man reclined and pensive. Chilling breeze
Around him seemed the leaves to rustle low
And near his shaking hand, within his reach,
A small decanter from whose neck a flow
Of laudanum seemed oozing to and fro.

The Man was reading from a parchment page
On which were stanzas, strangely moving, spaced.
He looked the very image of a Sage
The Spirit of the Poet's Word had known
For many years, whose company was graced
With genius of thought and converse fine
Whose images of fancy pleased the age
From which his intellect will ever shine,
And stir our equal visions, yours and mine.

'Is that your Ancient Rime you hold?'
Enquired the Spirit, drawing close,
As nearer now and growing bold
He touched the holding hand. 'Twas cold
As ice. The Man so slowly rose
And said, ''Tis Christabel I own,
Which you rejected, leaving me alone.'

'I wrote it for the Ballads Lyrical
But then rejection was my lot to know;
The Bardic verdict was inimical,
And thereupon the Muses fled my mind
Bereft, Poetic pictures future show
Not images sublime or shaped in stone,
No longer will entrance my fellow-kind
Nor visions paint, nor inspiration find.'

The Poet Spirit had no need
Of Answer to the former Bard;
His offered page he did not heed
Nor conscience did he feel to bleed
Remorse, inflicted by the shard
Reproof, but turned and slowly said
'I famous was long after you were dead.'

'My fame extinguished yours when still
Alive the World acknowledged me;
Unkinder men, reviewers, will
Keep silent pens uplift to kill
The reputation others see
Deserved by verses pastoral
And observations almost clinical.'

'But yet, know this, my long-time kin
Long after me, long after mine
Will come compilers, and within
Anthologies of verse, on sin
Or joy, on moon or on sunshine
May not include a Balladeer,
But surely will embrace the Marinere.'

'And Kubla Kahn the World will know
Far longer than some Peter will,
Or Betty Foy her son to show
Or Goody Blake and others slow
To intellect. A flowering hill
Or Derwent stream may keep my Name,
But Ancient Rime forever means thy Fame.'

The Spirit of the Poet's word appeared
Now closer to the former Bard he knew,
And closer now and closer still he neared
And took the hand that penned Dejection's Ode.
So cold. So cold. He held the hand anew,
And felt new life and warmth between his own.
'My Ferryman and I have distant rowed
And must return before the Dawn is shown.
Farewell, my friend, we leave you now alone.'

Then former Bard soft wept upon the sand,
For fame he once espoused, but threw away,
And tears of understanding on the strand
He shed as heard he now the Future's Word;
The verdict that his dreams would, come the day
Entrance the readers of another age,
When ranting critics fall upon their sword
While humbler men, emotive scan the page
Which for all Time confirms him as a Sage.

He turned and plucked the vessel by his hand
And deeply drank the opiate once again,
Then placed the never empty glass on sand
Where lately tears had fallen by the shore.
Then slowly to the Glade without more pain
Returned to sit where beeches cast their shade;
And then he wrote some lines, and then some more,
Of joyous days and friendship's beauty made,
When all life's tribulations were allayed.

Of days when he and Spirit of the Word,
In company with gracious, lively minds,
The Quantocks or the Lakeland fells explored,
Descriptions wrote for future stanzas bright
Of hills and trees and Nature of all kinds,
Of sunlight, shadows and the growing flowers,
When noonday rays appear the fields to light
With blazing torches in the summer hours,
And he and his had great poetic powers.

'Come, Ferryman of Windermere,'
Again commanded now the Word
Of Poet's Spirit: never here
Again, nor sonnet, ode, to hear;
The rower's effort once more spurred
Along, as darker falls the night
And on the sleeping leaves the dews alight.

'Come, Ferryman, another land
Must visit on the lightless Lake,
Another place, another Land
Must greet upon another strand
Before the Spirits new awake
To sunshine day and future Time
When our todays are seen to be sublime.'

Then through the mist a pastoral land appeared
Quite sudden, brightly lit with evening Sun,
And on the grass-green fields, seen as they neared,
A lady walking briskly through the green.
Though slightly built, she almost seemed to run
So urgent was her journey to the West
Where by the trees a cottage home was seen.
Her step was brisk, her movement quicker lest
The following rain might catch and soak her best.

'Come, Ferryman, row quickly now,
I must the lady see full soon.'
Then leapt the Spirit from the bow
Before the rower leaned the prow
On shoreland. Did the lady swoon
Or merely stumble by the door
As came the Spirit from the nearing shore?

The Spirit of the Poet's Word embraced
The lively lady by the cottage door,
Then shadows of the cottage them effaced
As hand in hand they lightly trod inside
To long converse on recent years and more
When intellect suspended Poet's mind
By indigence of efforts oft denied,
Whilst later years ambition ceased to find
Fulfilment, or the praise of humankind.

So long they spoke, so low their voices soft,
To share the days of criticism made
When moments pleased, or adverse comments oft
Required amendment by the Poet's pen;
Or sitting in the cottage orchard shade
The drowsy summer air invited sleep
And indolence embalmed all thinking, when
In fitful dreams the mind its treasures keep
And rarely through a cloud does logic peep.

And long and long they sojourned by the Lake,
And long and soft conversed of days now gone
When each the other's happiness could make
Complete, and minds together forged a dream.
'And then ten years no longer wisdom shone
But life became embalmed on Rydal Hill
And all our years of sharing life might seem
A memory which emptiness might kill,
Did not our words live on, and flourish still.'

''Tis true, my Brother, yea 'tis true indeed
That each we lived the other's life and made
A prompt awareness of the other's need.
And so while I, domestic, helped the home
And you, the former family renegade,
Became an honoured Bard, I with your wife
Allowed your fertile mind to distant roam
And pen the fragments of a rural life
Without the burdens of domestic strife.'

'And shared we all the pains of tragedy,
The children gone in tender years too soon,
The brother lost in perils of the sea,
The nearby friend laid low with mind disease
Long after predict by the gypsy rune;
We rode vicissitudes from year to year
And from their pains exquisite solace seize
In weeping company which shares a tear,
And binds the family to banish fear.'

'I must away,' the Bard at length declared,
'My journey scarce begun continues on.'
'Then think of me and of our living shared
So precious after banishment in days
Of early womanhood and childhood gone.'
'How could I easy Gift of God forget,
Who filled my thoughts as does a fire ablaze,
We shared a life fulfilled as few could fret
For greater worth, renewed forever yet.'

'Come, Ferryman, now quickly row,
Depart this place with sorrow dressed
And to my gaze a happier show,
For of a love I wish to know
That early years emotion blessed
And gave a love by war maligned
And kept apart a family assigned.'

So distant on horizon cottage sinks
And far from land the rowing Phantom moves.
On memories the Spirit lonely thinks
Of family he had, but that denied
By circumstance with conquest often proves
Impossible to thwart the plundering hordes,
Nor planned reunion may be misapplied
Should rise again the armies with their swords
To blight the land regardless of his words.

Then slowly, far to windward, seemed a land
To grow upon the vision, on the mind;
The hills with woods deciduous, unplanned
And riotous profusion, tree on tree,
The land seemed different, of foreign kind
As tropic jungles far to South of these
But thriving, temperate, as any be
With structured wilderness of Northern trees
Yet European in the drizzling breeze.

'Where are we now,' the Bard enquired
'Why bring me here, so far from home?
The woods, the trees, a place embowered
It seems in foliage rampant mired,
Scarce clearly seen beyond the gloam.
Why bring me here when I would see
My youthful love, and with her once more be?'

'This is the place, this is the land
Your journey made in yesteryear,
Beyond the tide, beyond the sand
The fields and woods of France grow grand
Again, not separate by fear,
Nor by repeated wars apart
Shall keep the first love of your Poet's heart.'

Then through the trees two figures dancing came,
A woman lithe and comely was the one,
The other by her side a child the same
In movement and in countenance so close
The image of her mother through her shone.
'Annette and Caroline,' the Poet said,
'I see again the one I early chose,
And then the one by other gently led
Beyond tomorrow, where we all are dead.'

The Spirit followed quick the dancing pair
And to their home remembered made his way,
Too little time, so short a dream to share
With sacred memories the days obscure
But none can lightly cast aside the day
When friendship means the world to you and me,
When love was shared, self-evident and sure,
As touch and glance from one to other see
Fulfilled commitments shall their loving be.

The Ferryman awaited in the cold.
No substance his the family alone,
For they have memories to share of old
When hearts were light with love and passions new,
When in the eye the mutual radiance shone
And dreams were made impossible to see
Fulfilment in a world afraid, askew,
No matter how the love so deeply be
Imprinted on the hearts of such as we.

The time passed slow, and cool the distant moon
Looked down as cold and slow life's sojourn seems,
But Spirit of the Bard appears not soon
To break the visit of a phantom day,
For who too soon would shed life's early dreams
Or brisk escape renewal of a bond
Which once was destined ne'er to fade away
And live forever with a passion fond
Until today reclaimed from the Beyond.

So mother, child and Bard their years forgone
Awoke again the love no wars can slay,
And in their ears were memories alone
To share, when Revolution tore the heart
From Nations worth a less endangered day,
When tyranny replaced a rule betrayed
By visions of a fairer, juster part,
But saw the world in consequence was made
The crueller far by random flashing blade.

'Come, Ferryman, I must away,'
So spake the Bard beside the oars,
'My Peace is made, we've had our say
And dreamed our dreams of yesterday.
We must away to further shores
And seek my worthy friend of prose
Who industry o'er pleasure often chose.'

So through the dark again they drove the waves
And long the journey seemed to each and one
While bent the rower as might galley slaves
In harsher days to quick the route to war.
So moved the flying boat as splashes shone
And further lands their modesty might keep
With Humankind and Nature yet asleep.

And there it was, the Hall of Greta named,
Transported here from Keswick to the North
Where lived a man in life by many famed,
A Laureate in deed for many years
Although in distant days his verses worth
By many less acclaim they had in life;
And yet a worthy man without the fears
Of penury, of living without strife
Supported not by one, but threesome wife.

He strode, a taller man than Bard was he,
Distinguished, aquiline and lean of frame,
Immaculate in manners, gentle see
His bearing as he greets the nearing Bard.
'Whom have we here, the man of future Fame,'
He smiled to greet the nearing ship to shore,
'The man whom Greatness will endow his name,
To whom I cast my wreath for evermore
Nor critics higher praise those gone before.'

The Spirit of the Word, the Bard, replied
With gracious bow and took the offered hand,
And each in arm, without a trace of pride,
Together strolled enraptured by the grace
Of company, and there upon the sand
Their footsteps mutual into the night
In wandered line made slow and measured pace.
Such former friendship set the world to right
And brilliant Minds as these the world alight.

Long time the footsteps wandered side by side
Along the shore, scarce lit by any light,
While thoughts of Madoc, Nelson all abide,
Kehama and Brazil with them are shared
Within their memories, as dark the night
Encourages converse of Poems writ,
Of diligent approaches, projects dared,
When Bards together read their other's wit
And scarce had need to change one word of it.

How soon, too soon, the conversation died
How dark, too dark, the hazy night so close;
With what emotion men have frequent sighed
To part from those admired and loved for long,
When mutual respect is not verbose
But puts succinctly what it has to say,
Or by a catechism sees no wrong
In those enchanted by a sunshine ray
Or those endowed with diligence to pray.

Thus spake our two pale Phantoms in the night
As turned their steps again to new embark,
The Bardic Spirit and the Laurel wight
Returned to boat and Ferryman alike
And slowly, slowly slipped into the dark.
The vessel with our phantom twain on board
As Laureate beholds the rowman strike,
And waves a parting greeting, not ignored,
As lifted deep emotions, spirits soared.

'Come, Ferryman of Windermere,
My heart uplifts, and yet my Mind
Still troubled is while we are here,
Still troubled by these memories dear,
I need a deeper peace to find,
Come row with me beyond today
And transport me afar and soon away.'

'Come, transport me to social days,
To days when youth and summer shone,
To days when Lakeland cattle graze
At Brathay: who shall sing the praise
Of family in grief now gone
To further shores far, far away
While we remember once a happier day.'

And so the rower and the Bard once more
To perils of the waters dark and deep
Moved out of sight of land and distant shore
To journey in their quest another page
Of former history, now fast asleep.
As soon a little island came in view
On which a mansion, seeming of great age,
Sat close to river murmuring anew,
And nearer yet the river noisome grew.

'I know that sound,' the Ferryman declared,
'The sound of rushing water Brathay makes;
How often have I sat, how often shared
The sound as through the portals of a tall
Cathedral heard when pealing anthem shakes
The columns. So on many a darkly night
I sat and saw the summer twilight fall
While he and I together, without fright,
Would share this Heaven's sound, devoid of light.'

This time together both the Spirit Bard
And Ferryman, his former friend and peer,
Alighted on the shore whose pine-trees guard
The rivers confluent from higher Lakes,
And to the mansion, brooding, with no fear
Made way. There at the door their friend and wife
Were welcoming with gesture pleasure makes
To see a warmth each had until their life
Disrupt became, and madness became rife.

But now, the pleasure gleamed from each their eye,
Such were they full of happiness and joy
The day the Ferryman near passed them by
But Theodora bid them pause awhile
And meet his new-found neighbour by the croy
Whose wife, Sophia, auburn, twenty-five,
A comely mother with a sunshine smile,
Already seven children, happy, live,
And for them all with tender care did strive.

Not yet for years the shadow blacked the sky
When sad delusions, paranoia, came
To blight the poet's spirit, mind awry,
Until asylum's walls oppressed his soul;
Then later yet the family in name
No more dispersed and pain their lives oppressed.
So she, Sophia, became the leading role
And kept alive the family she blessed
By being there, although in sorrow dressed.

But here, today, the sunlight flared again
As friends together shared a happier day;
The children in the garden played amain
And social converse filled the happy home
For many hours until from one did say,
'Forgive us if we journey from the Sun
For we have far to go, from far have come,
And through the Night of Death the hours run
Too soon, while we the Dawn of Life must shun.'

So sadly from this happy house depart
Our travellers of Night into the haze,
And many tears emotions keep apart
Before the final farewell is complete,
For they suspect the tragedy of days
The future would defile with wickedness
When one of them would leave his comfort seat
To live a life of misery, duress,
And no more share such homely tenderness.

Thus slowly, sadly sat the pensive pair
With numbness in their limbs and in their heart,
The future's tragedy neither would share
As Fate made mayhem with a faultless life,
But each might wish to abrogate a apart
Of Future's intent on the family,
And spare the tribulations of the wife,
Or conquer sadness with a homily
Inadequate to hear unhappily.

'What further visits must we make,'
Enquired the Ferryman at oars,
'Before the Living Dead awake
And we our rowing must forsake
Before the Sun horizon soars
Above, and we our parting share
Before the Sun emerges into air?'

'One more, one final visit yet
I must assign, I must pursue;
Row strongly now, no dangers fret,
For she I loved must not forget
Who owes her now my homage due,
For life and love was all to me
Whilst I loved her, and she my love could see.'

And then across the black and gloomy Lake
A flash of light transpirited the dark;
It seemed the very waters came awake
And rainbows shone in pairs far overhead,
And on a rocky headland, near and stark
There stood a female figure all alone,
A lantern lit beside her tilted head
From whence the light upon her clothing shone
While rainbows shined and then were swiftly gone.

The Bard, entranced, stood speechless with his friend
Before with measured step he climbed ashore,
And wanton ran the broken years to mend
When she lived on into a greater age,
While he with Dora, Kate and Tom, and more
Became the Firmament itself above,
But now he would in hope for age on age
Again his wife, his only lifelong love
Secure for future Time, and worship prove.

As met the pair, the darkness fell again;
The boatman, journeyman, sat with the tide,
And long conversed the married pair of when
Their happiest days at Dove with children blessed,
The Bard at peak of powers before there died
The impulse of immortal words to say,
When skills of word manipulation rest
And find no more the sustenance of day,
And Genius may pause, and penship stay.

'I will return,' at length the oarsman heard
Him say, 'and then together we will fly,
Will fly the Heavens as swift as any bird,
And spend Eternity beyond the Earth
Where Sadness, lonely, makes all men to die
And Winter's coldness bleeds the throbbing heart,
And Genius bereft, a dreadful dearth
Of talent fills the land, where perverse Art
Pretends, and Beauty has no power to start.

So to the cliffs and shore the Bard made way,
Behind, the wife he loved for many years
Stood quietly musing on this Phantom Day
When from the Past came an historic Bard,
A Bard for whom she now shed happy tears,
For he would come and claim her for his own
When from the Night returned. No sadness marred
Her joy, as he into the ship was shown
And each to other made their homage known.

'I weary now,' the Spirit of the Word
Declared, 'but you have rowed me through the night;
You have few words addressed to me,
Nor made complaint, nor e'er inferred
A discontent your labours to you be,
So tell me, Ferryman, and tell me right,
How know you all the lands we've seen
And rowed me where I've never been?'

'Good Spirit, I have known a while your song
And given praises to the World for you,
For I have known your words for years
And kept their moving beauty long,
And oft by phrases poignant moved to tears
Have loved the sentiments expounded new,
Your pictures of the rural wild,
The gliding stream, the smiling child.'

'For first I tried to show my love for you
In tender days, but shyness bade me stay
Afar from hero at Town End,
And years flowed by before I knew
The joy of pleasure I could not pretend
To be but other than a glorious day,
And days to come with mutual care
Enshrined by all who Lakeland share.'

'For you and I, we shared our joys of life
And wept together in its tragedies,
When Kate had sudden left us all
And Tom likewise departed strife,
We grieved as one, and shared the shouldered pall
And railed at life's, at death's, inequities
While I on Kate's last place, prostrate,
Entreated Heaven to ope her Gate.'

'As years went by we shared a family
Of friends, of wordsmiths seeking to bestow
Posterity on cameos
Descriptive, not too wordily,
To fire the interest of those who chose
To ride with us the chariot we know
Of language careful writ, alive
With sentiments on which we thrive.'

'But when I chose not to your friend espouse,
Your helpmeet, but instead found love and life
In humble farmer's child nearby
And comment made was to arouse
And then the coolness fell I knew not why,
Such cooling glances fell upon my wife,
And even more upon my deed
Because you thought her low in breed,

'Then was my love and friendship oft reviled
And soon forgot the praises which I made
To all the world awaking to
The simple song, the humble child
Of whom you wrote with sympathy anew,
Nor critics feared, reviewers not afraid,
You gave us images to dream
That lowly life may Holy seem.'

'Accuse me not; I know your words ring true,
I you rejected for no honest cause
And I will carry in my mind
The imputation I will rue,
Ingratitude I own: and can you find
Within your heart an injured pen to pause
And then forgive a mind austere,
Remorseful now, but cleansed of fear?'

'Indeed I may, I hold it not a sin
To disapprove of sentiments of love
Albeit out of social kind
Or felt beyond, or felt within
The social norm, rejected by the blind;
For only time commitment can disprove
Or show the truth of love and worth
Before the pair return to Earth.'

'But judgement sometime made by those who err
Themselves must carry lesser weight of scorn,
And those who know by whom accused
Themselves are flawed, becomes a spur
Their condescension by victims amused
And of its critics sentiment is shorn
Of all but mild intolerance
And of no deep intransigence.'

'I fear not from your faultless pen,' replied
The Bard incarnate seated in the bow,
'For juster you have been than I
Was often tempted, ere you died,
To paint your image, and your worth belie,
But now integrity in you I know
And recognise a lifelong friend
Who praises me from start to end.'

'The future will endow my words with praise
And laurel wreath around my neck will place,
But your facility with prose
Will also last, will also raise
The admiration of the one who knows
Perfection in the written word, and grace
In phrases, lines oft magical
And words descriptive, musical.'

'Come; cools the night, we Spirits are afar
From land we knew in carefree days long gone,
I'll row you to the Eastern shore
Where can we part, no words to mar
Our friendship through the decades gone, and more,
To places where we wandered, sunshine shone,
And all was beauty in our lives
And ever yet the memory thrives.'

'So let it be, so let us share the night
And drift the phantom surface of the sea,
And hold forever in our hearts
The Gratitude we shared aright
For each's gifts, for each's several parts
Of Genius the years will come to see
We each endowed posterity
And both enriched Eternity.'

Then drifted through the silence of the night,
As gliding ripples left the moving prow,
The slowly moving phantom ship
Two phantom men, an eerie sight
The one with oars outstretched and phantom grip,
The other sat in solitude bent low
As through the dark, the haze, the cold
Their memories returned of old.

And ere the dawning light to East appeared
The land was reached, the silent journey ends,
And from their places both alight;
They stand awhile, of dark affeared
Before they walk too boldly through the night,
'Then let us part for always, both as friends,'
The Ferryman declared aloud,
'As each to other be avowed.'

'So shall it be,' the Spirit of the Word
Agreed. 'So shall it be eternally.
We each had gifts to give to Man
The flowing phrase, the rhyming word,
And with our fellow written Sages can
Of moral good confirm fraternally
That beauty does not with the day
Nor with the stormcloud blow away.'

So turned they each apart with outstretched hand
And silent trod their each and separate way
As Dawn the mountain ridge revealed,
And early light shadowed the strand
At which their phantom ship lay now concealed,
While earth was waking to a Human day
Where Spirits are but Fantasies
And Sages are but Memories;
And so apart the Spirits to the Light
Gave way, as dying fell the Night.

ELIZABETH SMITH

Elizabeth, where can one start a Life
To praise which ended in adversity,
Cut off before ascending prime and powers,
And yet in short a time encompassed much:
Achieved a mastery of languages
Self-taught would be the envy of a crowd
Of lesser minds? But now you lie alone
At Hawkshead with its scattered sloping graves,
A tablet white of marble all to see,
The message plain for all Eternity.

'She talents great possessed and virtue high,
With piety was blessed' is all it says,
But not enough her life is thus endowed
With praise for what she was and what she did
Before consumption struck her to the soil
And died she out of doors on tented lawn.
So passed her life away before three score
Of years Life gave to her and then, too soon,
Her cultured gracious mind no longer stayed
Nor visions pious on her features played.

In Durham County was she born, six years
Beyond the start of Wordsworth's life, and then
To Suffolk moved when but a growing child.
From there her family, inheriting
Fair wealth, became the guardians of a Hall
Beside the river Wye, Piercefield its name,
And there began her quest for languages
For searches spiritual into the Word
Of God, whose Hebrew and whose Grecian text
She studied first, translated also next.

By year of her majority had been
Acquired all talents that her life possessed;
A fluent linguist in a list of French,
Italian, Spanish, German, Latin, Greek,
To which add Hebrew, Persic, Arabic.
Linguistics yet not all her talent shown
In studies philological. Her ear
Was musical, her skills in playing harp
The expert harmony of dulcet sounds,
Her homestead pleasureful with joy abounds.

And yet, accomplished and so privileged
A life was not to thrive, nor vaunt its skills,
For tragedy in life's progressing stream
Lay like a gin-trap by the rabbit's den;
Not just her wealth was mortgaged to the dawn
But health and life itself betrayed by time
Inopportune. In geometry and then
In algebra her mind excelled, so then
In poetry her talents bloomed and shone,
Extinguished only when her life was gone.

A sketcher of some talent, she could draw
From Nature with perspective's eye and line;
But Language was her first and chiefly love,
Translation her ability supreme
As when from German Klopstock's Life she penned,
And then from Hebrew changed the Book of Job,
A work so accurately done and near
To Truth that Hebrew scholars of the day
Described it closer to the Word of Time
Than any other Book of God sublime.

Yet with these talents, not a single word
Was published in her life. All came to print
When she was dead. Her Klopstock Life,
Her Book of Job, her Prose and Verse compiled
From fragments only then in memoir saved,
Appeared the world at large at last to show
How varied all her self-taught skills had been.
But ere the curtain fell the double pain
Of poverty and health declining, both,
Converted industry to doleful sloth.

Finance collapsed, the splendid Hall was sold,
The father forced to spend what little left
By purchasing Commission to the King;
And so abroad to restless lands subdued
By vagary or force, unhappy Isle
Of Ireland, whilst his family behind
Was left. First Patterdale embraced their home
And later Coniston adopted them,
And there Tent Lodge became their final place
A family of intellect and grace.

Tent Lodge, so called because upon that spot
Was pitched the tent in which her talents died,
As fevers, weakness, pallor took their toll,
The laboured breathing and the sweated brow,
Her final days one summer out of doors
As August warmed the mountains to the North,
Were spent with views resplendent to admire,
And meekly was accept her knowing fate
As on a morning sunlit o'er the hill
Expired her life, and passed her ebbing Will.

Scarce known today, shall we her life forget
Or cease in admiration to her praise,
The lesson learn that industry and toil
May make profound a talent latent laid,
No need for teachers who have intellect
Less well endowed, by pupils oft eclipsed,
If application and the love of words
May be enough a Genius to spawn?
Where are they now, whom such as we adore?
Or is her history to be no more?
Not in her life her accolade deserved,
Her memory with future love preserved.

JOHN WILSON

What better friend, what kinder man than this
Could men of letters through their life enjoy?
A brilliant mind, a wealthy merchant's son,
Ebullient in manner, but with this
A tender-hearted Soul and caring love
Of each his fellow man, as well of poets
And of all who loved the written word.
A father lost in youth endowed those left
Behind with comfort and sufficiency,
And him of words a vast proficiency.

He also was to make the Lakes his home
To be at hand the Lakeland man to join
And there he met his fellow Oxford man
Contemporary but such different fame,
Yet he would years to come by nom de plume
Retain his status and his eminence
In matters literary; while his friend
For years would be but little known abroad,
Until Confessions and his greater tales
By them most others' weaker effort pales.

He, like De Quincey, early saw the Bard
Of future Lakeland and his towering mind,
But not for him the quiet withdrawn affairs
Of academe. He had the energies
Of herds of oxen in a full stampede,
And in his youth was frequent patron of
Such arts as fisticuffs, of wrestling and
The driven horse, the wind-blown ship at sea,
Nor e'en the cockpit was averse to him,
Though we today eschew such sportures grim.

And rightfully described Athenian
By Ferryman of Windermere, was said
The versatility to then possess
Of Alcibiades, or Robin Hood,
Who o'er adversity not always won
But would at times succumb to stronger men
And take defeat without or rancour nor
Displeasure at his own humility.
A boisterous man good fellowship he loved,
Undisciplined, a genius he proved.

First winner of the Newdigate he was
Long 'fore Ravenna won the prize for Wilde,
But when his intellect was in full flow
He still led daring exploits out of doors -
As when first seen by fellow musing man
He was at 4.0 A.M. across the moors
On horseback in the dark in hot pursuit
Of rampant bull, with anger set to charge,
No thought his safety to secure, or save
His skin from challenging an early grave.

To any company he could adapt,
To any intercourse contribute make,
But early though aspired to Poet's crown
And volumes wrote of verse, now little read,
His brilliant future was as critic laid
In prose both virile and emotional;
A fluent and a rhythmic line he wrote,
Thus was his love of melody betrayed
In all he spread across a dazzling page,
Few writers better in that sparkling age.

Such scintillating man of quality
In wealth material and of the mind,
It was but only of a predict course
He would espouse the Beauty of the Lakes,
But scarce their happy state had been endowed
Than came misfortune and financial tears.
An uncle, guardian of his business life,
Incompetent his fortune lost: default
At best, dishonesty more likely cause,
And to his sun-blessed life gave chilling pause.

Two years of hardship pressed upon his purse
While creditors redemption sought from him.
'Tis said, and wisely so, financial ties
Do not enhance most friendships if at all,
But this, his mutual friend esteemed through life
Exception made; De Quincey, slim in purse
Himself, came to his aid and succoured him.
Most men acquaintances enjoy but few
Have friends to match, but Quincey loved his peer,
And each the other's talent did revere.

So when life's fortunes changed in later years
His home and purse together were disposed
To any need his friend might forthwith need,
And though his lifelong friend became in thrall
To opium, and lethargy thus brought
Into his mind to dull his seething sense,
This gentle friend encouraged and cajoled
De Quincey to at least abjure enough
To write his brilliant essays, some in Tait
While he remained at Blackwood's favoured gate.

In time his clearly able flashing prose,
His social presence on the Scottish scene
His just renown among the critics made
Its impact; he was rightly raised to hold
The lauded Chair he held for many years.
His later life in industry and toil
Exemplary in letters was displayed:
And year on year his friend he helped along
But would not leave his sacred Elleray
Where sunshine o'er the mountains breaks the day,
So both their alter years with worth endowed
The brilliant man society had praised
Worked out his life, his early promise proved,
And by his friends enduringly was loved.

CHARLES LLOYD

Who was this man, for whom the treasured earth
Threw down a carpet full of gold and tears?
He was by primogeniture endowed
The heir of bankers of indeed great wealth,
And Quaker childhood and a tutored home
Prepared him for a literary life,
Although he could not walk the cloistered Halls
Of privilege until apostasy
Allowed embracement of a Christian creed
Before the College walls acclaimed his need.

And yet so promising a life to be
Was tainted by inherited disease,
In later years his family to maim
And bring a happy edifice to earth.
But ere the tragedy unfolded, cruel
In outcome, came a span of years when joy
And talent garnered each with fruits, and when
In College days he met and wooed a girl
Both beautiful and with a manner kind,
None better would be suited to his mind.

And with his friend Charles Lamb he stayed awhile
To share the glittering company unique
Of Coleridge in his Somerset domain
Until, in illness, Coleridge nursed him through
To fuller health. The Bard had later mocked
His verse, and that of Lamb, with sonnets wry
And humorous, for which his recompense
Was laughingly a drug-hazed hero in
His 'Edmund Oliver.' So vengeful truth
Had claimed a friendship turned to solemn drouth.

The family would not his wishes grant
To wed Sophia who his passion shared,
So they eloped and made their love their own,
By Southey aided in this covert task,
And then a residence together made
At University at first, and then
Penrith became their home for brief a stay
Before they chose their future family home,
Low Brathay with its vistas by the Lake,
And there a happy homestead would they make.

So flourished they before the shadows fell
Upon their lives, and when De Quincey met
Their household on a rainy Lakeland day
All seemed in joy and happiness immersed -
A lavish income from paternal wealth,
A house with servants generously supplied,
A focus for the social scene for miles,
A home with several children blessed by now
Their mother, barely twenty-five, her hair
With auburn tinged, her youthful skin still fair.

And so the summer nights were lived away
With social joy and dancing on the lawn,
And literary men would join their sphere
And share the bounty they were pleased to give
In grateful thanks their happy state to own;
'So young and rich and happy, full of hope,
And with young children belted (now most dead)
And standing on the verge of labyrinth
Of golden hours' - while in the distant gloom
Betrayal 'gan manipulate their doom.

At first the signs and symptoms were obscure,
A mood swing here, an irritation there,
Depression then appeared, withdrawal next,
And early epilepsy came again
More frequent now, and then the paranoid
Delusions thrust their evil ill intent,
'Dull trampling sound of man or many men
Advancing with repeated threats to him
Or with accusings oft continual'
Would tread their soul-desponding ritual.

In hope of these debilitations to
Assuage he filled his mind with other things,
And to the book of verse he earlier wrote
With that Charles Lamb of critical acclaim
He added translates of Alfieri's plays
And published them, and later sent to print
His novel in two volumes, given to friends
But then withdrawn, in case the men he loved
Thought little of his talents or with ill
Regard might view pretensions with the quill.

And while his sister married Christopher,
The younger Wordsworth brother later to
Become the Master of a famous Hall,
His friendship with De Quincey ran so deep
That in the evening hours when troubled mind
Accosted him, and shadows fell upon
His soul, they both would sit beside the stream
Where Brathay from the Langdales streams above
And joins the Rothay, placid now in flow
Through Easedale, Grasmere, Rydal runs below.

And so the little river Brathay sings
Her song - 'the sound of pealing anthems as
If streaming from the open portals of
Some great cathedral limitless.' And then
'No stranger could I swift persuade belief
In it to be none other than the sound
Of choral chanting - distant, solemn and
Of saintly tone.' So shared De Quincey with
His friend whose future both discerned with fear
Was soon to grow into a tragic year.

'But sometime also . . . I have heard in that
Same chanting of the little mountain stream
An admonition of a different kind,
Less agitated, but a requiem
For happiness departed.' So it was;
Within a round of scarcely fifteen years
All came to wreck. 'Put not your trust away
In any fabric of the joys or roots
Of happiness derived from fellow men,
No, not of them, nor less of their children.'

'Love nothing, nor love anyone at all,
For thereby comes a killing curse one day.'
So bleak a message from their friendship flowed
And who can find to blame such sorrowed word?
Before the Regency had run its course
Insanity was evident, and so
The Bard himself, brother in law to him,
Drove South with him to fill asylum's void
While Dorothy to Brathay loaned her life
So Sophie might accommodate her strife.

Not all was lost, the mind not all destroyed,
For intermittent was the tragedy
And times there were when lucid moments lived
And even literary work was done;
So later works on London and on Pope
Were still accomplished 'fore the falling cloud
Enwrapped his mind again uncertain, cruel
And wanton with its now perverted grip
Until one day, no longer be endured
The brutal day, his freedom he secured.

But only by default; absconded he
And straightway to Dove Cottage made his way
To find De Quincey and entreat his help,
Then made their way, supposedly again
To hear the river Brathay sing her hymn;
At Ambleside late in the night he left
His long-time friend, no more to plead his case.
Not long it was before recapture came
And to asylum was he swift returned,
While friendship was cast off and brusquely spurned.

At length his mind improved and home he came
But briefly, then to France they made their way,
Sophia bravely faced the family's woes
The deaths of children and returning ill
Of husband's mind, once more incarcerate,
Until at last unhappy life was through;
In maison sante near Versailles he died
And lies there still, by wife was later joined;
As fortitude forced tribulations cease
'That morning brought him liberty, and peace.'

LAKES

From Paradise where Devon rivers flow
To grander hills and streams, which show
The harsher face that hardship used to know,
The Lakeland hills and mountains in the rain
May brood the sultry brow again,
Or covered high in mists where gods have lain
Upon the tops to far away survey,
We all await the sunshine day,
And thankful prayer the rambler high may say
To reach the valley in a fearsome flood,
Near lost among the clouds which could
His life endanger, clifftop o'er the wood.
And here for ages past the Poets lived
Not only Wordsworth here survived,
De Quincey came to praise the one he loved,
And Coleridge in the happy early years
Before reduced to wanton tears
And opiates turned dreams into the fears
Of nightmare; they and others shared the wild,
The great outdoors, the growing child,
And brought to Poesy descriptions mild,
For others to declare their written page
The insights of a kinder age
And show to all the greatness of the Sage.

POETIC PARADISE

'Whom have we here, who knock upon the door
Of Paradise Poetic, of a Life
Fluorescent in the balm of Poesy?
For here the Intellect, the Mind, and More
Subsume mere mortal Talents born of strife
Rejecting rules evoking Heresy
To win enraptured praise from hearts of Men
As they, uplifted, Nature praise again
And all is Sanctity within
Where Life Eternal may begin.'

'Who claims a living Fame with others here
That drum the Message through Eternal skies,
Where Metre, Rhyme and Pageant all contrive
To bring to words the colours painters fear
To splash the canvas lest the Image dies,
And what was dead appears to be alive?
Have you, Have you the verbal paintings made
Of which all counterfeiters are afraid?
What names can you present for Fame
And how to Fame may make your claim?'

'We all were Lakeland dwellers once a time,
In Somerset enjoined to all inspire
The origins of verse Romantic, wild,
When poetry both with, without, a rhyme
Ignited in our Souls a dreaming Fire
And gave to each the wonder of a child.
Thus in our writing more was said of good,
Of emanations from the vibrant wood,
Imaginings both bold and strong
As might such ponderings prolong.'

'So such your Fame, but what your Lives have been?
Fine dreams may soothe the literary heart,
Give comfort to yourselves, but not to all.
Your Names must be declared, your virtues seen
Before your Genius is told in part
To be a worthy thing that all may call
A blameless or a worthy span of days;
Or if not those, evoke at least some praise
Of kindness to your fellow man
Before indulgences began.'

'And when your Names I know, your Lives assess,
We will decide, if one, or two, or all
May enter here to join of former years
The best whom History, without duress,
Interrogated in her marble Hall
And found not wanting by illustrious peers
Were claimed by all, without serene reserve,
To be contributors prepared to serve
As well to bask in others' praise
And Fame endure for endless Days.'

'I am the oldest, and will speak for all.
My name is Wordsworth, Poet, Pastoral Man;
My taller friend is Southey, each of these
To which may many others also call
Complete a Man, and an Historian,
As well Reviewer, Critic slow to please,
A family Man beloved by all he met,
A Man, like me, who had his faults, and yet
Inspired in all a selfless day
Before his mind became astray.'

'My other friend is Coleridge, Genius
Is not too strong a word of him to use;
His Talents and his Mind are huge indeed,
And if his Life at times was devious,
And laudanum would oft his mind perfuse,
His character some days a bending reed,
He nonetheless lived Life, and gave his Love
To others with no wilful wish to prove
But other than a passion true
From which his human stature grew.'

'Your Names are known to me: we will begin
Interrogation of your Lives and Fame,
So Fortune and the Future jointly own
Your Minds, no claims obtuse, nor others' sin
Might cloud judicious praise, or to a Name
Attach demur, and separate a throne
Of Love Eternal from a lesser life,
As one might pledge unto a future wife,
All fealty from Now till Then,
And swear it soft, and soft again.'

'Who will begin his Soul to bare to me
And we who will decide his future Fate?'
Strode forth the tallest of the supplicants
And boldly said, 'I first of Travellers Three
Will lay my Work before you at the Gate
And be the first of we three mendicants
To brave your Scrutiny. My name to all
Is Robert Southey, late of Greta Hall,
My Life is yours to judge and weigh,
May your decision none gainsay.'

ROBERT SOUTHEY

'May I your life's biography begin?
Of humble stock in Bristol were you born,
A linen draper's son of modest means
Whose father died in debt, if not in sin,
And to your aid a maiden Aunt applied
Attention caring, whilst an Uncle spied
Your talents. From your parents were you torn
Although with caring, while your study leans
To matters of the pen political
And wordy stanzas, often critical.'

''Tis true, my Aunt Elizabeth was good to me,
And Uncle Herbert early saw my mind
And paid the fees Westminster School required.
But there a fervour grew, for I could see
The brutal faults which lay within its walls
And wrote a treatise in a text which calls
For end to corporal punishment, a kind
Of proposition critical, desired
To humanise the school: for this was I
Expelled; my intellect they left to die.'

'Again my Uncle, kindly man, gave me
The tutelage required to educate,
And though of Institutions now I held
Contempt, to Balliol my way did see
By application diligently made
To all their then requirements, and displayed
An early love of verse; did predicate
Such care for poetry and words which meld
Sensations in the Soul, an early poem
Was started there at length, and in proem.'

'That was your 'Joan of Arc' which made your name
Well known within two years. But while you were
Still in an Oxford life a visitor
Arrived. With Joseph Hucks one Coleridge came
And you and he and others all contrived
Invention of a social creed, derived
From universal equity and where
Each has the other as inquisitor
Of universal welfare, where no blame
Is native born, and where all are the same.'

'It Pantisocracy was called by all
And to this concept of a common good
Aspheterism we did add as well,
To emphasise that ownership should fall
On each and every one of such a band,
And each and one, all working hand in hand
Might not require excessive wealth, but should
To each declare, and to himself should tell
The needlessness of avarice is clear,
And wealth is those whose loves and lives are dear.'

'And so we hoped one day a group might live
In green Kentucky with these aims in mind,
And later Susquehanna was our goal
Where ran the deer and herds of bison thrive;
And man in commune might his fellow love
In equal partnership, and stars above
Might shine their blessings on a newer kind
Of human grouping, each aspiring Soul
In honest toil for common good would strive
His utmost, and we all would feel Alive.'

'But with these thoughts were others not so bland,
The rise of revolutionary thought
Accompanied this communal ideal
And anti-Monarchist might others brand
Our fervour for the cause of Liberty,
Equality and for Fraternity,
Before the tyranny of France was bought
By blood and murder, and no man might feel
The freedom anarchy usurped of Breath,
And even followers were done to Death.'

'And then our band of men became aware
Of female company and social whirls,
The Fricker girls, all five, became our friends
And Burnett, Lovell, all their charms would share
Until the ranks of converts greatly grew
And all the sylphs knew us, and we them knew,
And even mother joined converted girls
In scheme to travel West to earthly ends.
And so we dreamed of Poetry and Life
Where friendship communal abolished strife.'

'Then why and how this prospect not endure?'
Enquired the Gateman of our Paradise.
'Where how such sentimental leanings failed?'
'The hearts of family became enured
To our fond hopes, I was disowned of wealth
By both my Aunt Elizabeth in stealth
And Uncle Herbert's manner turned to ice,
With anger both their countenances paled
By thoughts of revolution I espoused
And those who dreamed with us in common housed.'

'Without the funds required my friend and I
Made talents subject to a baser need;
We turned to journalistic skills for pay
And lectures Jacobinical to ply
A trade to raise the emigration fees
That we would need to sail the westward seas,
And sank the aspirations of a breed
Of future Poets planning for the day
When Art not gold would drive our motives high
And thoughts majestic dream the evening sky.'

'Thus now from College left for Poet's life
And called a firebrand revolution man,
The sweet delights of womanhood so close
Were breathed, that Robert Lovell took to wife
One Mary Fricker, and myself a vow
I made to Edith, that for then and now
We would through life, as close as any can,
Be permanent, the one to each have chose
None other, though the Siren makes her play
And sings alluring songs of love all day.'

'But 'fore I to the altar trod the way
My Coleridge friend a Fricker third had wed,
For he took Sarah of that comely house,
While I, when we would from the Church straightway
Proceed to Portugal where Herbert had
A Church for emigrees, the pale and sad
From England left behind, the living dead,
Who by default another land espouse
And then regret their sojourn, daily sunned,
As they their families and friends have shunned.'

'By now with Coleridge cooled the friendly days
But came I back to England now well-known:
Although our Pantisocracy had died
My Poetry had won substantial praise,
And so to industry in verse and prose
My latent talent and my vigour shows
Its future course, a future pattern shown
Where industry succeeds through efforts tried,
But inspiration rarely rears its head
As though imagination now were dead.'

'And then as simmered on the perverse view
And tyranny in France disgust evoked,
Our views were tempered by their evil deeds
And with the bloodshed further horror grew
Till we no more talked loud of Liberty
When what it meant in murder all could see
And France's degradation. Now provoked
To make a married living, meet the needs
Of future family, I tried the Law
But soon abandoned this, its failings saw.'

'For short a time in Dublin went to stay
And serve the Irish Chancellor abroad,
But only shortly stayed away from home
And then returned to publish come what may,
My Thalaba, by many viewed askance
And named by me a metrical romance
And not an epic none but they accord,
But metres rambling made the visions roam,
Too high! Too high their aspirations led
'My days (through books) are passed among the dead.' '

'By now with Coleridge reconciled anew
Misfortune came with grief to haunt my mind,
Our Margaret had died so soon before
We took our path his company to view
And there at Greta Hall we shared his home
While he and Wordsworth Lakeland landscapes roam,
And fertilise each other's verse in kind
Encouraging the Muse with rural lore
While in my library my studies bloom,
Prolific is my prose, half fills my room.'

'By now my Patron William Wynn is placed
In Parliament his brother to enjoin;
His brother and himself by voices strange
Are with amusing anecdote embraced
As 'bubble and squeak' their voices low and high
Respectively, and were he not too shy
The Speaker's Chair was thought he might purloin,
But solemn tasks sound oddly in a range
Of voice more like a gelding's than a man's,
Or like a lady hid behind her fans.'

'While Coleridge fled and Malta life began
The household came to me for full support,
The widow Lovell (he had long since died)
Together with her son, the Coleridge clan,
And later when 'The Friend' has slow expired
And opium the turgid mind had tired,
Three families at 'Ant-hill' of a sort
Dependent on my work were not denied,
My industry painstaking in Review,
To Madoc added other works anew.'

'So toiled I day by day and hour by hour
Protean works to orate to the air,
I only of the triad paid my way
By penship spite of criticisms sour
And even Byron, cynic as he was,
Described me as the only man who has
The title of complete a literaire,
And who might hope from him a word to say
That was less jesting than his sonnets strong,
Or complimenting of another's song?'

' 'While Southey's epics cram the creaking shelves'
He jaunty made a diatribe of me,
But works of mine found better praise than his
And who for him would prostitute themselves?
'Oh Southey, Southey, cease thy varied song
A Bard may chant too often and too long'
He wrote; perhaps he penned with jealousy
Because ere long the Laureate came along
And Scott declined the crown by Pye released,
By then for prose his love of verse near ceased.'

'My works will stand in time a tested place,
My Life of Nelson, Wesley, not the least,
Though Paraguay, Kehama may not last
In man's affection, or the least efface
The effort in their waking; time may show
My life and work to those who want to know
Was greater now the cynic's word has ceased
To crucify a fellow Bard, and past
Effusions critical from Scottish Lords
Cannot erase the cadence of my words.'

'In later life at Greta sadness grew
As son, like daughter, died while yet a child,
And ever then depressed, successively
I waved aside both 'place' and offers new
As Editor of Times, and thanks to Pitt
A Baronetcy offered, think of it!
To me the firebrand democrat, once wild!
I bid it go with thanks dismissively
By now resigned to live declining years
In comfortable ease, protect from tears.'

'When George the Third his final illness met
And I his life decided to acclaim
The chance arose to Byron's pride enrile
By criticism of his work, and yet
The rest our lives we spent by other spurned
Though each the other oft his verses learned,
And efforts each the other tried to maim
If not by humour or by jibe revile
Then in reviews or prefaces to write
Belittled summaries or captions trite.'

'Too young he died, too young for such a Bard;
We did not hate, although abrasive oft
Of each's literary toil, but on I sped
Upon the path of Glory and too hard
Might strive immortal memory to earn,
For such it is that Poets often yearn
To claim posterity endowed, aloft
The laurel wreath is borne before their head,
While they with humble Grace affect disdain
For Glory, though they worked for it amain!

'Then further tribulation struck my home:
My wife began to lose her thinking mind,
So many years, so many years of love
Had held our lives in hope for years to come,
But not to be, the future's day had palled
And to declining years her Soul was called
Until in middle life was misaligned,
Her thinking and capacity to prove
A logical sequence. Within three years
Her life and mind had gone, immersed in tears.'

'A petty phase of pleasure was to me
Bequeathed beyond these tragedies. I met
Again and married Carole Bowles, but ere
We settled in a life mature to be
A solace to us both, my mind astray
Was trailed beyond tomorrow for today.
And soon declining years, slow moving yet,
The downward path was treading, share by share,
Until I could no longer years recall
Nor memory find where tears of sadness fall.'

'And in the end how shall my life reveal
Its industry, and its emotions feel?
Could be my Story of Three Bears alone
Survive for decades hence in others' mind,
While epics in confused a rhyme atone
For all, but cease for any human kind
To lift the souls of any but the blind.
This is my Life, do with it what you will,
Posterity may grieve, nor think me ill.
So Gateman, be my Judge, if so you can,
My Life has ended well, as it began.'

SAMUEL TAYLOR COLERIDGE

'Now Coleridge, what have you to say
That would admit you to our Paradise?'
Enquired the Gateman. 'Light the day
With how your mind began its journey long
And then bewitched and dazzled by a throng
Of impulses too seldom wise,
Made less a mark upon the mind of Man
Than others less than you who strove to scan.'

''Tis true my honoured Gateman, yea
'Tis true, my life did never full achieve
The promise it began; the day
I joined my father's tribe, number thirteen
I was of his offspring, by mother seen
Of less a brood; Papa did grieve
An earlier wife who daughters three him bore,
Whiles I was number ten, eight brothers more.'

'My father was a self-made man
Both theologian, Latin scholar wise
Who both the local Grammar ran
As Headmaster, and Vicar above all
Of Ottery St. Mary, where landfall
Begins to nearby sea as flies
The crow a fewly miles before the breeze
Of southward Channel blows to western seas.'

'My early years, immersed by older
Brothers and, I felt, rejected by
A mother treating me the colder
Than the rest, I refuge took in love
Of elder sister Nancy who would prove
My closest confidant; though shy
She shared my every fear and little joys,
Protected me from more rumbustious boys.'

'While first at school my vivid mind
Predicted how my future world might seem,
With nightmares would my thoughts unbind
The terrors of imaginings too bold
And fearsome dreams would cleave the winter's cold
And dark, nor e'en the lucid dream
Might solace give to my too fervid brain
Which willed the tranquil pasture lands to gain.'

'So thus at night my screams awake
My brothers and my sister frequently,
And even in the day might make
Fraternal friction, as when I surmised
A brother was more favoured, was more prized
Than I, and him I fought boldly
Then ran away and stayed a frightened night
Beside the river, rescued by a Knight.'

'Sir Stafford Northcote rescued me,
My frantic parents still abroad at dawn,
And for a while they pampered me;
And now the Grammar School became, though small,
My alma mater, but its charm would pall,
And when my father died was born
The need to have a further learning life
Elsewhere, afar from home and bereaved wife.'

'And so Christ's Hospital became
My final school and nourisher of mind;
It might be harsh, and yet its name
Lives on for me, for there my talents thrived
And not for years returning home I lived
Except for journeys of a kind
Too transient to fix the family bond
Or even Nancy know my feelings fond.'

'There later was I joined at school
By one who later life remained a friend;
Like me he followed close the rule
Of college law, intent to see the day
When he could learn the Poets, nor betray
His yearning nor to Churches wend
Reluctant steps a tranquil life to live,
But intellect submitted, scarce alive.'

'Charles Lamb he was, and is, too sad
That vagaries denounced his poet mind
And bode him in a moment mad
Renounce his Bard ambitions heretofore
And afterwards, and yet his prose the more
Was recognised of deeper kind
Than mine might by posterity acclaimed
Be thought less formal, yet perhaps less maimed.'

'And so awoke in me the Muse
Of Poesy, and verses schoolboy penned,
And there I heard the crashing news
Of Bastille's fall and, teenage fervour roused,
Republicanism is now espoused
And shared with Tom, my schoolboy friend,
But best of all, his sister, early love
Of mine, but not in later life would prove.'

'But often sickness would my days
Prevent from formal round of classic toil,
And then, alone, the poets praise,
Identify with Chatterton, the boy
Whose paranoia bled his life of joy;
So I like him would be disloyal
And cast aside the classics for the praise
Of poets who might pen the favoured phrase.'

'And though by fevers and by pain
Of joints immobilised I none the less
Though week by week in bed was lain,
An exhibition gained for College life
So leave the school, and leave its petty strife
For manly things, but life's distress
Was not to spare my dearest sister nor
Her helping smile deprive me evermore.'

'She died: the one I dearly loved,
The one my ragged childhood helped along
The one by injury unmoved
Were it to her, but for my sake would fight
My corner with a vigour and a might
Surprising. Never more her song
Would sleep my drooping head like lullaby
Nor take my childly hand to stem a cry.'

'So start the Cantab. life at last
A grieving brother and a budding Bard;
Uncertain what to do, but fast
To live in London when I can, and wild
Became my ways and thoughts, no longer mild
Opinions, but manners hard,
A Jacobin at heart, upheaval moves,
Not known tradition nor prior order loves.'

'And yet this pride for France's coup
Did not endear my friend, his sister's, love
For me, she looked on me anew
And cooled our teenage ardour in the sun,
So scarce my wildly life had yet begun
For oft to London would I move
And whore the leisure hours to soothe the pain
Of unrequited love, then whore again.'

'A happy prospect this, if I may say,'
The Gateman interrupted, by the way,
'Is this an application we should hear
For Paradise, or are we waiting here
A London Club, Bordello, to decide
To grant the applicant, or him deride,
His naughtiness rebuke, excuse revoked
Before in explanations weak 'tis cloaked?'

'I bid you Sire, I bid you Sire
Refrain the mocking jest my tale to jibe,
'Tis hard enough, my humble Squire,
To thus abjure a former life of woe
And to the world my sinnings all to know
In such a way; your diatribe
Offends my simple story, told enough
With hesitant displeasure; Be not rough.'

'You blame me worthily and true,'
The Gateman now confessed to all about
'Forgive me, now that I do rue
My thoughtlessness. Please carry on your tale,
The substance is not mine to judge nor rail
At others is not mine to shout,
For I, no less than you, have things to hide
Nor would I wish by you my acts to chide.'

'I thank you, Sire: and here my tale
Takes on a strange romantic phantasy,
For thus my love began to pale
And, so confused, impulsive made a stand
Against my past, against a future planned
To publish verse, apostasy
It seemed when Ode to Fortune had been writ
To throw it all away, the whole of it.'

'Yet this is what I tried, believe
It or believe it not, the budding Bard,
The published Poet, planned to leave
His College and Republic views behind
As well his former love, and those unkind
Of his outrageous life. 'Twas hard
To cast it all aside, but this I did
And subjugate my mind to others' bid.'

'The Fifteenth Light Dragoons became
My home, although such life was not for me,
My fellows scarce believed my fame
Endowed with classic talents far above
Those owned by any peers, e'en those that love
The written word, they could not see
Me cast as lancer, horseman, man of steel
And sword, a man so plainly meant to feel.'

'At last my brother George, who all
My life gave succour to my vagaries,
Arranged to pay, and then to call
Me out beyond the fenced walls of war.
How so the dread Dragoons were led so far?
With others they made histories
Which had my mind unhinged, declared a bane,
I left the Army labelled thus, 'Insane'.'

'Returned to Jesus, gated, then
Released and then to walk the hills of Wales,
But on the way to meet the men
Who would with me and others later drive
Ideas communal, when all might strive
An equal life to live, where pales
Authority before equality
And each and all apportion parity.'

'At Oxford stayed with Southey, one
Of life's dynamic and disturbing minds,
Rebellious and fervid, lone
A voice almost subversive then, but now
Conservative as any else; and how
Might such as he throw to the winds
The Pantisocracy we both conceived
Nor my Aspheterists should be believed?'

'Thus we with Lovell, Burnett, Fricker
Girls, and other close-knit friends of then
Considered emigration quicker
Than our purses could subscribe the fare,
And so our talents flourished everywhere
To journalism gave the pen
And lecturing political contrived
To keep ourselves until fortune arrived.'

'Of course it never did; but young
And foolish were we then, and gullible,
And now we mutual had sung
An interested song to sirens near,
So Robert shared with me the sisters dear
And both together voluble
Became our talk, as Mendip hills we paced
And then to Nether Stowey steps retraced.'

'By now the dulling mood of Halls
No longer can my roving mind contain
As with the winter interest falls
On academe, and so I leave behind
The University with vision blind
To soaring words of my refrain
And with support direct my future life
To writing first, and then to take a wife.'

'And so it was the following year
I first met William of the towering mind,
And quarrelled with a friendship dear,
So closing down our emigration plans,
But consolation came by reading banns
To Sarah am espoused in kind
And we to Clevedon move a loving home
And share the rural hills where red deer roam.'

'A year beyond the signs are seen
Of future trends; although my friendship
Was restored, the rift has been
An augury of trials yet to come;
I nurse till death another friend at home,
Continue with poetic penship
Various, and then decide no more
To journalism mix with Nature's lore.'

To Nether Stowey near my friend
And early patron we repair whilst I
Prolific write and talents bend
To works sublime, a time when blooms the Bard
And ventures joined with Lamb and Lloyd, but marred
By later jesting made not by
Malicious or demeaned intent, and yet
Invokes an umbrage now I wish forget.'

'But Ballads Lyrical is now
Together planned with Wordsworth, such a time,
And there to him I now can show
Completed Ancient Mariner who will
My name establish and my Fame instil
Into poetic lists of rhyme
Immortal. Now my course is set to be
A man of letters with a vision free.'

'And as the Church Dissenting made
An offer for my preaching skills again
The Wedgwoods, who to them had prayed?
Annuity bestowed to me allow
A life of letters to henceforth follow
And this distressing choice made sane
By competence at least for short a time
Enabled me to turn again to rhyme.'

''Twas at the Church of Wem the news
Had reached me of this saving grace for me
And Hazlitt, William, saw my ruse
Of bending to a shoelace loose attend,
And so to hide emotion from a friend,
But still a youth he didn't see
How man by subterfuge his feeling keeps
Controlled, from moistened eye he furtive peeps.'

'Already I had tried the sweet
Embrace of opium two years before
When pain in face, and pain in feet,
Provoked the help of laudanum to use:
And pain relief with pleasured sense to fuse
A dangerous admixture bore
A warning of the future and decline,
When subsidence to apathy was mine.'

'So with a new felt freedom sailed
With Wordsworths to a German sojourn make
But quick their company had paled
And most my time was spent immersed in Kant
And other metaphysicals who rant
The strange idea, and wake
The logical with dull determined tread
While I, a Poet, phantasise instead.

'The century was ebbing now
And mixed the fortunes of its final year
My Berkeley died, and I allow
His passing not my plans to throw aside,
But when returned to home rejected pride
A barrier makes, a little fear
Arises in our married previous joy,
And with such little grieving for the boy.'

'But then my friendship is restored
To Southey and through Southern hills again
We share an out of doors accord,
And then to Lakeland with the Wordsworth pair
A walking tour enjoy, its pleasures share,
And meet their family, and then
Their Sarah see and fall in love for life;
By now have faded feelings for my wife.'

'And Daniel Stuart offers me
A prize so many would surrender glad
Their souls or lives to own, to be
The Editor of Morning Post is mine
If I accept, but brusquely I decline
So certain am I, scarcely sad,
To cast aside a steady writing trade
In hope of future fame by verses made.'

'And so we follow Wordsworths North
And live at Greta Hall, with them at Dove,
But when is questioned now the worth
Of such as Christabel and late in day
Its contribution spurned and turned away
I find a solace and a love
In Sarah H. and opium, the twain
Who will become for me a future bane.'

'And so together Nature and
The wild terrain we study all year round,
And mark the flowers on every hand,
The changing light, the clouds oft rushing by
On distant journeys through a purple sky;
But illness stalks my frame, the sound
Of self-made indolence by opium made
Until of future days I shrink afraid.'

'So William, Dorothy and I
To Scotland wend, I'm sure my health to aid
But as in Germany I sigh
To be alone and walk the rugged ways
Where on my brow the calming weather plays
A solace. Preparations made
To break the stifling bond of unloved wife
I seek abroad to live another life.'

'By diligent appraisal of
Things military, naval and indeed
Political my talents prove
Of value to Commissioner abroad,
My recognition and esteem has soared
In Malta where my early meed
Is Public Secretary, acting, though
Sir Alexander Hall my limits know.'

'But still the opium I take
Too often and too liberal for sense
And little verse of value make
Now I've become a bureaucrat instead:
One night, methinks, believe the Muse is dead.
And then at last a recompense
For industry in public life I turn
To home again, to where emotions yearn.'

'But time and distance let alone
Our temperaments have from my wife excised
Our former closeness, now a stone
Descends upon her attitudes to me,
And I would fain from her be ever free;
So more I live with Wordsworths, prized
For literary help from me to him
Whilst he and Dora grant my every whim.'

'And more and more I dote the while
On Asra, and her services impound,
And daftly wallow in her smile
Obsessed and smitten like a doting boy
Until unfilled the passions sour and cloy
Close friendship, and a mind unsound
Continues with addictive acts absurd
And warning voices wise are never heard.'

'But always restless journeys oft
I make to London, Bristol, meet with friends
Who hold my intellect aloft
In their esteem, and once again I stay
In London where the Institution may
My lectures, he who them attends,
Astound and mortify according to
My mood, the audience sometimes all too few.'

'Returning to the Lakes, the Friend
I now propose to launch, but badly planned
My contributions tardy send
Until, less thirty volumes long, collapse,
As most expected, comes. Maybe, perhaps
If drugs less frequent came to hand
And diligence did not by opium spoil
Success had been rewarded by my toil.'

'Despised now by all I knew,
By Asra, Wordsworths, wife and Southey all
Lost patience; Basil Montague
An offer kind to live with him had made
And so I left the Lakes, and not afraid
His home to join, he had the gall
To let me know of Wordsworth's warning voice
About my style of life; I had no choice

'But to reject his home and live
With other friends of long-time happy days,
And so to journalism give
My talents; for the Courier often write
And lectures on the Poets, penned at night,
To London intellects, with praise
Sometimes received, on other days confused
By opium I keep them all amused.'

'At last Crabbe Robinson, a friend,
And Lamb, both saddened by the Wordsworth rift,
Assist us to our friendship mend,
So in our later days our feelings turn
Again to warmth, if not once more to burn
With fervour, or the soul to life
To former heights of shared and genuine love
When days of Genius our Spirits move.'

'Between my lectures, writings, there's
A play at Drury Lane, with some success,
But illness dulls finance affairs;
And more and more my health declines and falls
And friends' concern by self-indulgence palls,
Nor would I put to them duress
To aid my weakness in declining years
Nor scorn the welfare of their hidden fears.'

'The years now growing hard for me
With illness and dependence creeping on
And never was my age to be
A tranquil time, although Biography
Was not in print and those who wished to see
My welfare, even Lord Byron,
Arranged assistance for declining days,
Despite no real amendment of my ways.'

'So further illness struck, at last
My surgeon Gillman's home became my own,
And eighteen years were happy passed
With him and his who sought my ills assuage
And nursed my final years through every stage
Of pale adversity, alone
I should not be, nor lonely pass the day
And he would shield me till I passed away.'

'Those happy years, content when well,
When all the literati of the day
Would come to me, beneath my spell
Would fall, and dine the evening light to shed
Before, exhausted, all would fall to bed
Entranced by all I had to say,
If not the port assists their dozing eyes
And lie content asleep at Dawning's rise.'

'So poems were collated, lectures
Given, and early works rewrit again,
Whilst all the Surgeon's well-meant strictures
All too oft by subterfuge betrayed,
Until struck low by illness and dismayed
That I of life enough of pain
Had seen, I thought another journey far
Was now o'er due, and passed beyond the bar.'

'There, Gateman, there's a restless life for you,
Is this the kind your Paradise might own,
Where flights of fancy through the teardrops flew
And convenants, conventions, equal slew,
But above all the human Spirit shows
Where love of Life and Nature equal glows?'

'It shows, my friend, indeed my friend, it shows.'

WILLIAM WORDSWORTH

'Now William, let us have your life long tale,
Nor spare the details of a Poet's life.
We know the reputation which mankind
Bestowed upon you in your later days,
But tell us of the struggles prior to this
Which marked your path to recognition just.
We wait with interest upon your word
And will not of its content be denied.'
So spake the Gateman with encouragement
As each and all their ear turned to his words,
Nor any sought remove him from the crowd
Of eager listeners to the supplicant
For true Eternal Fame among his peers
And for acceptance as Immortal Bard.

'Good fortune's bounty, north of Lakeland hills
Beyond the sleepy stream, the bubbling rills,
Our household gave a privilege to each;
For born Attorney's second son was I
In Cockermouth, my father legal arm
Supporting Sir James Lowther's reach
Of total power as far as eye
Can see beyond the Derwent's charm
Helped steer as Agent his o'erbearing ship
Of local Monarchy with feudal grip.'

'Our household flourished in these Northern climes,
Nor hint of any adverse future times
Disturbed our early days. It did not last,
For barely eight years old my mother died
Too young, too young. My father, dull and dour
Dispatched us all to Penrith, cast
On grandparents who justly tried
To make a second home and bower
For my three brothers and my sister loved
So dearly, till she also was removed.'

'And so to other relatives was sent
Our dearest Dorothy, our family rent
By plans domestic and expedient.
We saw her not at all for near ten years.
Within five years my Father also died
And so became convenient
A separation fraught with tears,
But while grandparents bravely tried
To fill the void misfortune had applied
Our Uncle Kit did little but deride.'

'But fortunately soon I went away
To Hawkshead School, and spent the happy day
At this a Grammar School of some renown,
While homely lodged with sympathetic host
Who fostered us in term-time and allowed
A freedom few in childhood own.
And there our boyhood, sun or frost,
Was to the fields of Nature sowed
And Mrs. Tyler, gentle loving heart,
To early manhood gave enchanted start.'

'So often before school on fine a day
I would round whole of Esthwaite make my way,
And oft at evening, or into the night
Explore the wild and hilly lands abroad.
Such happy years and days of scholarship
Preformed my love of Nature, light,
Of shadow, of the birds that soared
Above the cliffs, and comradeship
That shares such joys, which make to be alive
The senses tremble and emotions thrive.'

'And after hours of school alone would roam
The pastures and the rivers close to home,
The clustered forest and the hidden dells,
All full of life, of movement and of light.
No day the same, no season might repeat
The patterns on the green-grey fells,
Nor ever less the soul delight
As youthful gaze such visions greet,
Not squandered by the child's observant eye,
As form the fragments of a happy sigh.'

'By dint of toil and application now
I reach a necessary goal, and go
To Cambridge at St. John's, and there at first
Do well. But then corruption rife I see;
The crawling clergy, fawning sycophants
As pilgrims with religious thirst
Attempt a chosen one to be,
To powerful men are supplicants,
Preferment sought on eager shuffling knees
And seek like slaves their Master's whim to please.'

'And so my guardians looked at me askance -
And even more when I escaped to France.
I made it clear no honours course would ply,
Nor interest in future Church career,
But more and more I idled life away
Or turned a deafened ear or sight
To relatives who seem to fear
My future seems a dismal day,
But heady mood of change across the sea
I feel and empathise, nor wars foresee.'

'I see a Nation throwing off corrupt
A tyranny, my studies interrupt
To share the hope that such might be at home,
And all the edifice that I despise
Might likewise be displaced by better men.
To France with eager footsteps roam
And praise the wishes of the wise
Who leave the Royal courtier's den
And take up arms to free the poor and weak
From bondage which has always bound the meek.'

'But most of all a comely maid I met
Who, though a Royalist, in manners set
With gentleness and blooming womanhood,
Now taught me language, and a good deal more;
Behaviour irresponsible was mine
And after months when wisdom should
Have cooled the mind, our sense restore,
I left Annette, the heady wine
Of Paris did I aimless drink alone
While she, with child, laments that I was gone.'

'And while I supped this wine of insane times,
Before as yet the tyrant's evil crimes,
Annette my daughter bore and daily hoped
The coming clouds of War could not prevent
A longer contract with her hopeful Bard,
And dreaming that we all eloped
From savage times the quiet rent,
Reality her hopes hit hard
As wartime loomed, and tyranny's advance
Brought mayhem to the tranquil homes of France.'

'But I a listless, purposeless, and all
Too prospectless a Soul, and still in thrall
To image of a literary life,
Enhanced the dream by publishing some verse
Of rural scenes; and then my fortune changed,
Two school friends, neither with a wife,
One with poor health, the other worse,
A tour in Somerset arranged
And sought my company. And so agreed
I little knew they would secure my need.'

'Although my father had bequeathed on death
Substantial fortune, most he did bequeath
Was debt to him from Lowther - mad and bad.
For years the debt was never paid while we
In poverty were scorned by those in trust
Our education paid, but sad
It made us all their pride to see,
Our relatives, who knew they must
In future years our joint inheritance
Defray today's outlay to circumstance.'

'By now we had, rejoicing, seen again
Our dearest sister, robbed from us in pain
For years, and she and I at Windy Browe
Our friends the Calverts join a little while,
Then as the younger, Raisley, is more ill
I stay my love for him to show
And nurse his quickly fading smile
And failing tender years instil
A hope he knows his mind cannot sustain
But trust compassion will reduce the pain.'

He was the first to trust my future worth
And pledged his bond that when he left this earth
A generous bequest would aid my cause.
In early ninety-five he died with me
And kept his word, the legacy was made.
Such fortune drifting ways gave pause,
No pressing need for pupils be
My now and urgent plan, or stayed
My hopes to live a life of verse and rhyme,
Nor sacrifice it for all future time.'

'To London then and friendships old renew
Including one with Basil Montague,
And plans and offers made adopt a scheme
The widower's son in Dorset to emplace
And tutor him, with Dorothy to live,
And there above the sea to dream,
Poetic images embrace,
In rural happiness to thrive,
And so we did; and then at Bristol greet
The brilliant Coleridge, and his circle meet.'

'And this propitious meeting all our lives
Would change, although as Coleridge lecture gives
On theme Republican and radical,
I see his Genius as man of words
And meet his friend Southey, who's even more
Rebellious and prodigal
Than Coleridge is; and crossing swords
In verbal interplay am sure
Their views are similar and close to mine,
And from poetic eyes their talents shine.'

'And thus the seeds were sown, horizons yet
Unknown to us our tumbled thoughts beset.
Our common purpose inspiration finds
Whilst Southey, Coleridge, Fricker girls embrace
Both literally and with their future aim
Of Pantisocracy, our minds
Become enchanted by the grace
Of rural splendour and the same
Regard for rural fancies, beauteous hills,
For rivers, caverns, woods and distant rills.'

'And so we each in Quantock hills excite
The other's visions with the urge to write;
As Southey marries and to Lisbon rides
My Dorothy and I with Coleridge plan
Our several and ethereal refrains
We share the light, the hum of tides,
The rural solace summer can
The senses drowse, the vigour drains,
The shades of night, the light upon the corn,
'Twas there our common images were born.'

'From former discontent our Dorset life
We leave behind, join Coleridge and his wife,
And see through his and Dorothea's eyes
The rural beauty day by day we share,
The bedrock of ethereal refrains
And images proselytise
And share the convert's newborn care
For what imagination gains,
And so our Ballads Lyrical were planned
And guided each one's mind by other's hand.'

'Uplifted thus, to Germany we make
A threesome journey, there must Coleridge break
Our little band, his German studies there
To follow on his own. And on return
Again we three together tour the Lakes,
A happy omen can we share,
A vacant cottage cannot spurn
As Providence our future makes
A future nest, a home we all may love,
Available is made the cottage - Dove.'

'And so Dove Cottage, bulging full of souls,
Becomes a hive of life, and rapid rolls
Momentum of poetic fantasies
Until when Ballads are renewed, declined
His Christabel, he feels a slighted man,
Belittles his own qualities
Compared to mine, becomes resigned
To set aside what he began -
To seek immortal fame as future Bard
He now rejects, and seeks no such reward.'

'As meagre peace with France creates a pause
In war to be a future troubling cause,
I go to see Annette with future plan
And she without demur agrees to be
No more in hope my future life to claim.
Such sacrifice few angels can
Agree no more their partner see,
Nor him in future ever blame
Nor smile as child around her household plays
Nor with his mutual help its childhood raise.'

'But such she was, Annette, my firstly love
And through her sacrificial life would prove
No common parent, nor demeaned her pride.
With her consent I now a tryst pursue
With one whom all we knew since as a child,
And to Dove Cottage as a bride
My Mary Hutchinson is due
To bring her gentle manners mild
And make our home a family at last
Where our most favoured years were happy passed.'

'Though evil Lonsdale died in eighty-six
'Twas not till now his honest son would fix
Intent to honour what he owed us all,
But now at last commitment has been made
To debts repay as redress for the past,
But still delays our due windfall,
So frugal are our clothes arrayed
And simpler yet our day's repast
And so I empathise with poor and weak
And through my verse their humble praise I seek.'

'Though Coleridge lived, supposed, at Greta Hall
For most his time he kept us all in thrall
At our Dove Cottage, though his former friend
Now reconciled, alike to Lakeland and
To Greta made his way; but my reserve
To Southey would not warmly bend
Since with the critic's evil hand
Our Ballads would from him deserve
A false appraisal and the critic's curse,
And so of him I ever though the worse.'

'So blissful days, though simple in content,
Engulfed us all, and grandeur would prevent,
But more the cloud of worry 'gan to form
As Coleridge now more laudanum imbibed
Than was for any illness, real or nay,
Required, too much above the norm
In dose and frequency prescribed,
More indolent from day to day
Becomes despite our ever strong support,
While he the atmosphere for all makes fraught.'

'And so to Scotland Dorothy and I
Decide to take him, Trossachs or to Skye,
To try his growing ills to better solve.
But shortly he departs from us again
To plough his journey northward on his own,
While we our tour with firm resolve
Continue both on hills and plain
Until our steps to Scott make known
Result in welcome as our road leads past
And meet the man who penned the Minstrel Last.'

'And on the way to Scotland stop to see
Carlisle Assizes where we all agree
To pause and see a trial, Augustus Hope
The name that Hatfield gave himself before
He evilly deceived the comely Maid
Of Buttermere, until the rope
His fraud and forgery restore
An angry justice swiftly laid
Upon his head for mercenary crimes,
A fatal sentence as the Church bell chimes.'

'But Jury's wrath was less upon his head
For technical offences such as led
To his arrest. Their anger was inspired
By sordid tales of wronged young women left
In parlous state deceived by him in love,
And thus revenge in them was fired
To make amends for maids bereft,
And so his other misdeeds prove
A hanging matter by the Carlisle wall
Where Borderers had previous felt the fall.'

'Then Coleridge, restless, off to Malta goes,
The need obscure, the motive heaven knows,
And all seems calm and happy till the news,
The devastating death of brother John
Who drowns in Channel seas as sinks his ship,
His first command about to cruise
To Indies, and so sudden gone
We all are dazed; the trembling lip
The sobbing sigh no respite to our grief,
Nor tears in torrents gives our hearts relief.'

'No longer is our idyll full of thrills,
No longer walk the hallowed Lakeland hills
We shared with him, nor laugh the summer days,
Nor doze in Autumn's orchard side by side
Or glide the boated Lake in morning light
Nor seek a fine poetic phrase
As by the rippling stream we ride,
Nor smile as moonbeams glimmer bright
Across the Lake; instead a shuddering chill
Afflicts us all, and bodes the future ill.'

'We plan to move from Dove Cottage, the pain
Of poignant memories a constant strain
On all our minds, but news of Coleridge rare
Appears, and scarce the letters with his plans.
So work continues and the Poems in
Two Volumes is abroad; beware
The two sour critics, Jeffrey pans
My verse and Byron, man of sin,
Does likewise and my work puts to the sword,
And few are those who speak a kindly word.'

'The awful Jeffrey wrote no word for years
That justified a life above his peers,
But he in vicious tones, immersed in hate,
Wrote criticisms vile of better men,
He shabbily indulged in ridicule
In order to the work berate
Of able Bards whose rainbow pen
His sepia mind with minuscule
Imagination always will be less
Than those he scourged, sole purpose to impress.'

'You need have not a worry on that score,'
The Gateman intervened in humoured voice,
'He is not here, nor ever like to be!'
At this the listening throng the silence rent
With merry laughter and convulsive mirth
And nodded heads approving of this view,
For all despise the man who cannot do
But impotent himself makes others squirm
To falsify his own pretence to power.
'So critics sometimes show their lesser selves
And even Hazlitt mocked my rural themes
With a hint, mayhap, of jealousy it seems.'

'But one there was who early loved my skill
And never would my talents speak of ill;
He was De Quincey, master man of prose
Like Coleridge with a mighty mind indeed,
And fitting was it he would join our lives
And occupy, when Wordsworth goes,
Our lovely cottage where the seed
Of my best work was born and thrives
The master for two decades more in Dove
Which we, and later he, had come to love.'

'But we moved on to Allan Bank, surprised
When Lowther (Lord) our family apprised
Of partial purchase of, in Patterdale,
A property for us. Perhaps by now
The Lowther conscience had been pricked into
An act he felt would not entail
Apology, nor need bestow
On us the long-time measures due
By keeping all our family for years
In poverty, and constant anxious tears.'

'And so at Allan Bank the work goes on,
A Poet's work is never wholly done,
And I continue to extol the humble man
In verses ridiculed. And Coleridge starts
His Friend, with frenzy and in chaos writ,
Continues as it thus began,
Precocious child to all imparts
A message with a sombre wit;
But opium, procrastination, and
Ill-health portends an hour-glass short of sand.'

'The next two years are sad indeed for all,
The Friend no longer thrives, as 'gins to pall
His literary progeny, and then
The Asra Coleridge dotes upon rejects
His cloying presence welcome now no more.
She leaves. The author's wilting pen
No longer copes with his projects.
The publication fails, no words restore
His now and future drug-dependent life,
And now forever separate from wife.'

'He leaves with Basil Montague to live
Until the warnings I to him did give
About his drug-dependency are spread
In injudicious words, and so he goes
Instead to faithful Morgan for a while.
Although our friendship might seem dead,
Through Lamb, Crabbe Robinson and those
Who wish us well and have no guile
A reconciliation is achieved
And both of us are happily relieved.'

'But love once lost is never to return;
No longer can extinguished flames reburn,
And for a while our home becomes displaced
To Parsonage in Grasmere, damp and drear,
And there a double tragedy awaits
Our household. Little Kate, who graced
Our Cottage, loved by all, and dear
To us, expires. But hungry Fate
Not satisfied must then our Tom destroy,
The doted girl child followed by the boy.'

'The happy carefree days when all rejoice
Have died, and now is dimmed the Poet's voice.
We leave for Rydal Mount the grieving home
A better day our future to secure.
And fortune once again upon me smiles
As Civil office will become,
And stable future will assure
An income, though it many riles,
From Stamp Distributor appointment made
By largesse of the Lonsdales, I'm afraid.'

'But now De Quincey by a servant girl
An out of wedlock child conceives, the churl;
And growing love of opium impends
Addiction. These I cannot truly stand,
The love-child pricks my conscience of my own,
The opium a life portends
As indigent, unstable and
A future rolling ever down
The slope to destitution and despair,
When numbed the brain oblivion must share,'

'But when the Coleridge Biograph appears
In print, at last a sea-change sheds the years.
Belated recognition overdue
By all except a few becomes a tide
Of better will toward my written words.
Admittedly there are a few
My pompous prefaces deride
And bare again their flailing swords
With strictures of my methods and my style,
But now poetic praises bring a smile.'

'In later years my fame is gathering pace,
At last my Duddon sonnets given grace,
Acceptance, and some praise. The tide has turned.
A growing life of recognition starts
With accolades in London and by friends,
No longer by their humour spurned
The critics' vitriol departs
And jest sarcastic also ends;
But late the grudging homage still by they
Whose blinkered views they cannot cast away,'

'But now the sad decline we all must see
Begins its decremental slope. To me
And mine so also comes the pain of age.
The household of my hearth begins to fail
Whilst Poets die around me one by one.
First Keats expires at tender age,
Then Shelley, Byron, Scott the pale,
And then is Coleridge swiftly gone
Who though a Genius flawed inspired my aim
To be a Bard, as he espoused the same.'

'Then Lamb, and then beloved Sarah dies,
And on her death my Dorothy becomes
A mental invalid. James Hogg, all know
As Ettrick Shepherd, now is next away
While I live on to bask in later praise.
And then the powers that be endow
A Civil List award to say
They will assist my later days.
Then finally the Laureate is mine
When Southey dies, to end his mind's decline.'

''Tis sad to live when all around you die
But you live on, alone, and venture 'Why?'
Although for decades I had looked my age
Plus twenty years a certain rugged build
My health had kept secure, perhaps by life
Abstemious, devoid of rage,
With rural gentleness was filled
And succoured by a faultless wife;
So eighty were my years when Death my days
Fulfilled, no longer on the Lakes to gaze.'

'My Life is yours to judge, my Poetry
Mankind's to analyse and seek to blame
If so he must. Of none am I ashamed.
Pedantic, yes, and pompous prefaces
I will admit, but with the burning flame
Of Coleridge to uplift my early Soul,
The steadfast love of Nature sister formed,
And loving household to support my work,
Undying recognition by the like
Of Coleridge, Quincey, Wilson and of Scott,
My talents bloomed beyond what I was worth
To my own judgement, when the Muse spoke forth.'

There came a pregnant pause; the throng
A murmur issued round the lighted Gate
'I thank you Gentlemen, your Song
Has all our Bards Eternal held in thrall,'
The Gateman said. 'Lest I pre-empt my Friends
We will consider supplications all
Unless by acclamation is your Fate
Agreed.' He turned the growing crowd to call
To their attention and their wish invite -
'No better Bards than these our Souls delight.'

'Agreed, agreed,' the Phantoms said,
And murmurs rose from Spirits one and all,
'We hail these Bards now they are Dead,
Nor any Critic's word our view transcends,
None worthier than these our company
Could join, or in our Bardic world be friends;
Their vibrant verse will not our senses pall
Nor we think less of them for future trends -
When Poetry has neither rhyme nor scan
And they write prose who never verses can,
When Poetry, so called, is only prose
And authors lines adjacent interpose
A space to make a subterfuge of verse
And claim it 'modern style', or even worse.'

'Please join our World,' the Gateman said,
'We are all Living, though we all seem Dead.'
And so they passed the Gate to join the Light
Of Poesy, perpetual Delight.

While back on Earth the Lamenteer
A tribute reads for all to hear,
'Why is he gone,' the tribute says,
'While we lament his passing days,
Herewith accept eternal praise.'
As to his muse the Poet prays
And sees beyond the Lakeland haze,
Nor aught for him presents a fear,
Across the Lake a Phantom steer
A Phantom Ship, in pair appear
Pale through the mist, approaching near -
The Ferryman of Windermere.

WORDSWORTH
TRIBUTE

Why is he gone, the Man who loved the Muse,
While we, the many grieven by his loss
Dissect his life, and pry into his mind
To gratify our thirst, and ever fuse
His Life with Poetry of thoughtful kind?
For Ages will determine, should they care,
That He the laurel crown of All should wear.

Why is he gone, whose words provoke our tears
Of understanding, and embalm our joy
Of natural and simple things; for days
Of Spring and Autumn equal loved? The years
When envious critic, witless, cruelly says
He was a 'Dull disciple of thy School',
We know the envious rantings of a fool!

And we, his twice centennial readers, now
Accept the province of uncommon mind,
Which lowly gave a dignity to man
Not blessed with privilege or wealth. We know
The vernal message 'all the Sages can'
Impart more surely than the sonnet's sound,
And hear within an empathy profound.

For us, the dreamers of another age,
He was no 'mild apostate of the Poet's
Rule,' as quoth poetic craftsman George.
For us he was both Poet and our Sage
Whose pen, whose sister, and whose mind could forge
A sculpted image of a greater sense
Than we might know, what e'er the recompense.

For he, chastised by cruelling a word
'Who both by precept and example shows
That prose is verse, and verse is merely prose,'
Could ne'er himself enwield the cynic' sword,
And the one Poetic beauty knows
By verses blank, humanity imbued,
Made others' rhyming stanzas palely crude.

He was by Coleridge and by Quincey loved,
And rightly was by Southey often praised,
While those Romantics, dead before their time,
Wrote lines of him, and by his verses moved,
Themselves wrought greater miracles of rhyme
Than were they capable of forging, lone,
Because upon their verse his influence shone.

Millennia may pass horizons deep
And mere technology the senses dumb,
But images sublime the Lakeland Man
For all of us awakes the dreams of sleep,
While Paradise entrusts, to those who can,
The memory of him to laud, to keep
The finer things of human Soul and Mind,
And ne'er betray the humble or the kind.